Halloween

words&pictures

To Susan, in thanks for your friendship and sound advice,
and of course for your endless enthusiasm! — N.D.

© 2025 Quarto Publishing Group USA Inc.
Text by Nancy Dickmann
Illustrations © 2025 Laura Borio

Laura Borio has asserted her right to be identified as the illustrator of this work.

First published in 2025 by words & pictures,
an imprint of The Quarto Group.
100 Cummings Center,
Suite 265D,
Beverly, MA 01915, USA
T (978) 282-9590 F (978) 283-2742
www.quarto.com

EEA Representation, WTS Tax d.o.o., Žanova ulica 3, 4000 Kranj, Slovenia.

Editors: Alice Hobbs and Jackie Lui
Designers: Clare Barber and Mike Henson
Associate Publisher: Holly Willsher
Production Manager: Nikki Ingram

ISBN: 978-1-83600-126-3

9 8 7 6 5 4 3 2 1

Manufactured in Guangdong, China TT052025

MIX
Paper | Supporting
responsible forestry
FSC
www.fsc.org
FSC® C016973

Halloween

Nancy Dickmann

illustrated by
Laura Borio

Happy Halloween!

My name is Luna. It's fall,
and all the leaves on the trees
are starting to turn orange
and yellow. This means that
my favorite time of year
is nearly here:

Halloween!

Halloween is spooky,
but it's lots of fun. And this
year will be extra-special
because there will be a full
moon on the same night.
My name means "moon,"
so that's perfect for me!

Today, I'm riding in the car with my family.
That's my brother, Oliver, next to me. Mom and Dad
are in the front. Our dog, Rafferty, is in the middle.
Isn't he cute?

We're on our way to the pumpkin patch. When we get to the farm, a big red tractor is waiting. Oliver is so excited—he loves tractors! We all climb into the trailer and find seats on the bales of hay. Then the tractor pulls us all the way to the pumpkin patch.

There are so many pumpkins! Most are big and orange, but there are green ones and white ones too.

Mom helps Oliver and me choose a few. We load them onto a wheelbarrow to take them to the car.

Back at the farm building we have a snack, then we head for the corn maze. The corn is so tall—even taller than Dad! We take a few wrong turns but finally find the way out. Phew!

It's only a week until Halloween! Today after school, Oliver and I are making decorations. We use old newspapers and sheets to make ghosts to hang in the yard. Our cat, Midnight, thinks she's helping!

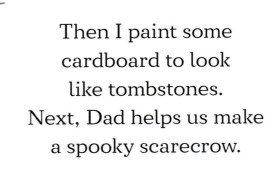

Then I paint some cardboard to look like tombstones. Next, Dad helps us make a spooky scarecrow.

It's nearly dark when we finish. Mom turns on the purple and orange lights. The front yard looks amazing!

11

On Wednesday, my friends Camila, Ava, and Anthony come over after school to work on our costumes. We're all going to be spooky skeletons this year.

Mom bought us some really cool glow-in-the-dark white fabric. Camila's good at art, so she draws the bones.

Then Anthony cuts them out and Ava glues them to black shirts and leggings. My job is making a mini costume so Rafferty can be a skeleton dog!

GLUE

13

On Friday afternoon, I take my pumpkin to Camila's house. Her dad is an artist, and he has lots of tools for carving pumpkins.

First, we have to scoop out all the seeds and stringy stuff. It's slimy and kind of gross! Then we draw our patterns on the pumpkins in pencil.

14

Camila's dad shows us how to use the little saws to carefully carve our jack-o'-lanterns. It's hard work, but lots of fun. Then we put candles inside to see how they look!

Saturday's going to be a busy day—we're hosting a Halloween party! Oliver and I put away our toys and help clean the house. Then we hang up paper pumpkins and fake cobwebs.

16

Once we're done,
Mom bakes pumpkin
cookies with Oliver,
and Dad helps me make
candy apples.

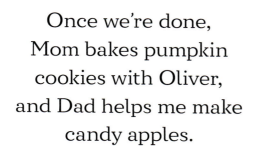

I push a wooden stick
into each apple, then
Dad dips it into the hot,
red sugar mixture.

Anthony comes over to help me
with the props for the party.

We want it to be really spooky!
We peel some grapes, and they
feel just like eyeballs. Then we fill
a bowl with cold spaghetti
to feel like brains.

Anthony shows me one of his favorite Halloween recipes. We cut pastry into thin strips, then wrap it around hot dogs. Once they're baked, they look like mummies. I can't wait to eat them!

It's party time! Lots of neighbors and friends from school are here. Some of Oliver's friends came too. Everyone is wearing their costumes.

We take turns putting on a blindfold and sticking our hands in the "eyeballs" and "brains." Gross! Then we play games. Oliver's favorite is pin the tail on the black cat. Everyone has a great time. It makes me wish that it was Halloween already!

On the day before Halloween, Oliver's preschool is having a trunk-or-treat celebration. We put on our costumes and pick up our cousin Asher—he's coming too.

In the school parking lot, everyone has their trunks open. Lots of them are decorated with pumpkins and skeletons. Mom stays with our car to hand out candy, and I take Oliver and Asher around. Their bags are full by the time we're done!

It's Halloween at last! I get up and put my costume on—I can wear it to school today. Camila and I walk to the bus stop together. All the houses on the block have their decorations up.

After lunch, everyone
goes to the school gym for
the costume competition.
Camila, Ava, Anthony,
and I go on stage together
in our skeleton costumes
and do a little dance.
We don't win, but it's still
a lot of fun.

This is it—Halloween night is finally here! I can see the full moon shining through the window. I don't really believe in ghosts or zombies or werewolves, but I still love Halloween. It's fun to dress up and pretend, and the candy and parties are the best part!

Ding-dong! There goes the doorbell. It's Ava and Anthony with Camila and her dad. We're all going trick-or-treating together. I grab my pumpkin bucket and we're ready to go!

It's so cool walking around the neighborhood in the dark and seeing all the decorations. Lots of other kids are out on the streets. And they can't miss us—our skeleton costumes really glow!

At each house, we knock on the door and say, "Trick or treat!" Then we take a piece of candy. Mr. Robinson on my block always hands out candy corn, which I love. After a "Thank you!" and a "Happy Halloween!" it's on to the next house.

Before long, all of our buckets are full. We go back to Camila's house and empty them out on the table. Then it's time to swap! Ava doesn't like peanut butter, so I swap some gummy bears with her. I trade Anthony a chocolate bar for some more candy corn.

Then Dad comes to pick me up—it's a school night after all. I tell him all about trick-or-treating and make sure to brush my teeth really well. Then it's time for bed!

Fall is my favorite
season, and Halloween
is a big part of that!
But it's more than just
the candy—I love it all.

Halloween is a great
chance to be creative. I like
coming up with new ideas
for decorations, costumes,
and pumpkin designs. I also
love sharing all of our
Halloween traditions with
family and friends.

Now I just have to wait a year for it to come around again . . . and I already have some great ideas!

Happy Halloween everyone!

How Halloween Began

Some Halloween traditions, such as trunk-or-treating, are very modern. But this holiday has a long history that goes back thousands of years. During that time, it has evolved from something a little more serious into the spooky, fun festival that is celebrated today!

SAMHAIN

Most historians agree that Halloween has its roots in an ancient Celtic festival from Ireland and Scotland named Samhain (pronounced SAH-win). It was one of four main festivals in the Celtic calendar, and marked the end of the harvest season and the beginning of winter.

People believed that Samhain was a time when doorways between worlds opened. This meant that spirits, fairies, and the souls of the dead could come into the human world. People lit bonfires and put out gifts and offerings to keep these spirits happy, so that they would do no harm.

ALL HALLOWS

In the 8th century, Pope Gregory III set November 1 as the date for the Christian festival of All Saints. It was a day to remember and honor all the saints of the Christian church. It was also known as All Hallows, and celebrations began the night before, known as the eve. Our modern word "Halloween" comes from "All Hallows' Eve."

Ghosts still come out on Halloween, but they're just costumes!

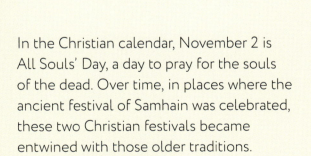

In the Christian calendar, November 2 is All Souls' Day, a day to pray for the souls of the dead. Over time, in places where the ancient festival of Samhain was celebrated, these two Christian festivals became entwined with those older traditions.

Halloween Traditions

When you think of Halloween, you might think of witches, ghosts, and skeletons. Or maybe you think about carving pumpkins, dressing up, and going trick-or-treating. There are a lot of different Halloween traditions. But where did they come from?

JACK-O'-LANTERNS

The first jack-o'-lanterns weren't pumpkins—they were turnips! An old Irish legend tells of a man called Stingy Jack who was cursed to roam the night hundreds of years ago. All he had was a lantern made from a carved-out turnip with a piece of burning coal inside. At Halloween, people made their own versions to scare away Stingy Jack and other evil spirits. Pumpkins didn't grow in Ireland, but when Irish immigrants brought this tradition to America, people starting using pumpkins instead.

> Pumpkins are ready to pick in October—just in time for Halloween!

GHOSTS AND SKELETONS

There are plenty of ghosts, skulls, and skeletons to be seen at Halloween. Since its earliest days, Halloween has been the time of year when the spirits of the dead feel closer than ever. Bones and skeletons have been a symbol of death for centuries.

HALLOWEEN COSTUMES

The tradition of making Halloween costumes goes all the way back to Samhain. People worried that evil fairies would try to kidnap them, so to confuse them they put on masks or dressed as animals or monsters when leaving the house.

TRICK-OR-TREATING

During the Middle Ages in Britain, poor people would knock on doors on All Souls' Day and offer to pray for the dead in exchange for food or money. In Scotland, children went "guising," where they would put on costumes and go door-to-door. They'd be given treats in return for singing or reciting poetry. Irish and Scottish immigrants brought their Halloween traditions to the United States, where they eventually turned into the trick-or-treating candy festival that exists today.

Make a Pumpkin Piñata

Enjoying candy is a big part of Halloween for many people, and this colorful piñata is a great way to make sharing fun! You could hang it up at a Halloween party and let your guests take a swing until it breaks and showers candy down on everyone. Or if you can't bear to break it, you can enlarge the hole, add a handle, and use it for trick-or-treating!

Your piñata doesn't have to be a jack-o'-lantern. Why not paint it white and then use black paint to make it look like a skull?

YOU WILL NEED:

- balloon
- old newspapers
- large mixing bowl
- about 5 oz flour
- water
- orange paint or orange crepe paper streamers
- black paper
- scissors
- craft glue or tape
- candy, for filling
- string

DIRECTIONS:

1. Blow up the balloon and tie it off. Make it big enough to hold plenty of candy!

2. Cover your work surface with old newspaper and then mix flour and water in a large bowl until you have a runny paste. (You can also use craft glue diluted with water if you prefer.)

3. Cut the remaining newspaper into strips about 1 inch wide.

4. Dip a strip into your paste mixture, run it between your fingers to remove any excess, and then drape it across the balloon.

5. Repeat step 4 until the balloon is fully covered with overlapping strips. (Leave the knot of the balloon uncovered.) Let it dry overnight.

6. Repeat steps 4 and 5 three or four times until the papier-mâché balloon is nice and solid.

7. You can either paint your piñata orange, or you can use crepe paper for a more authentic look. Take a roll of orange crepe paper and cut slits into one side to make a fringe.

8. Glue or tape the fringed crepe paper in overlapping rings around the piñata until the whole thing is covered.

9. Cut eyes and a mouth from black paper and glue them on.

10. Ask an adult to pop the balloon and enlarge the hole at the top (big enough to fill it with candy), then add a string for hanging.

11. When you're ready, hang the piñata up and take turns hitting it with a stick until it breaks and the candy falls out.

Make Your Own Banana Ghost Pops

Halloween wouldn't be the same without a few ghosts, but there's no need to be scared of these deliciously sweet frozen treats! They're quick and easy to make, and they'd be great for a Halloween party spread or as a spooky snack.

YOU WILL NEED:

- 4 bananas, fairly firm
- about 8 oz white chocolate (either chips or a bar)
- mini dark chocolate chips
- shredded coconut (optional)
- 8 craft sticks
- microwave-safe bowl
- cookie sheet
- wax paper

DIRECTIONS:

1. Peel the bananas and chop them in half. Cut on a slight diagonal so that each "ghost" has a body that ends at an angle.

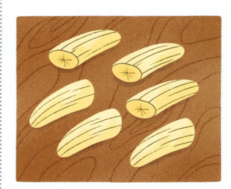

2. Push a stick into the bottom of each banana half.

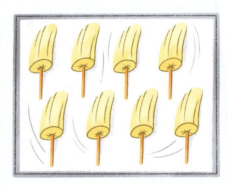

3. Line a cookie sheet with wax paper. The sheet should be big enough to hold all the bananas, but small enough to fit in your freezer. (Use two separate trays if you need to.)

4. If you're using coconut, spread it out on a clean surface, ready for coating the bananas.

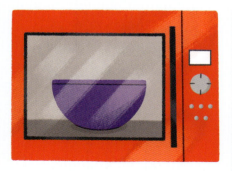

5. If your white chocolate is in a bar, break it into pieces and put them into a microwave-safe bowl. If you have white chocolate chips instead, just pour them into the bowl.

6. Microwave the chocolate in short bursts of 15–20 seconds, stirring between each one. (If you microwave it for too long, the chocolate will burn.)

7. Once the white chocolate is melted and soft, hold one of the bananas by the stick and dip it in. You can use a pastry brush to make sure the entire banana is coated in chocolate.

Maybe we should call these "boo-nanas!"

8. If you like, roll the banana in coconut until the outside is coated.

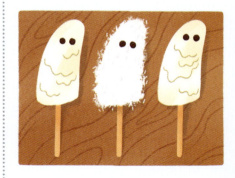

9. Add mini dark chocolate chips for the eyes.

10. Place the ghost pops onto the cookie sheet and stick them in the freezer for a few hours.

11. Once they're frozen, enjoy your sweet and spooky treat!

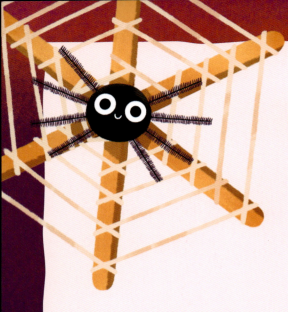

Make Spooky Cobweb Decorations

Are you scared of spiders? You'll see plenty of fake ones at Halloween. Why not try making your own spider decorations?

YOU WILL NEED:

- 6 craft sticks
- craft glue
- string or twine
- black and white paint
- air-drying clay or craft dough
- googly eyes
- black or purple pipe cleaners

DIRECTIONS:

1. Arrange the craft sticks like a six-pointed star and glue the center ends together to hold them in place.

2. Once the glue is dry, you can paint the sticks white, or leave them plain—it's up to you!

3. Take a long piece of string and glue or tie one end to the center of your "star."

4. Starting in the center and using the string, work your way around the "star." Each time you reach a stick, loop the string around it before moving to the next one.

5. Once you reach the ends of the sticks, tie off the string and use any extra to make a loop for hanging your cobweb.

6. Snip the pipe cleaners into eight short pieces to make legs for your spider. Roll a round spider body out of air-drying clay or craft dough, then poke the pipe cleaner legs into it.

7. Once the clay has hardened, you can paint it black and glue on googly eyes, then add a little smiley mouth. Glue the spider to the center of the web and hang it up to spook your friends!

COBWEB "SNOWFLAKES"

If you know how to cut white paper into snowflakes, you can make cobwebs the same way! Start with a square of black paper and fold it diagonally three times to make eight segments. Using a white pencil or chalk, draw on lines like in the picture below, then carefully cut them out. Unfold your paper to reveal a perfect spiderweb!

Remembering the Dead

Modern Halloween is celebrated in the U.S., U.K., and Canada, as well as in other countries where its traditions have spread. It's mostly seen as a fun occasion to celebrate all things spooky.

But Halloween began as a time when people felt closer to the world of the dead, and many different cultures have festivals with a similar purpose. These occasions offer a chance to remember and honor those that we've lost.

DÍA DE MUERTOS

In Mexico and Latin America, people celebrate Día de Muertos (Day of the Dead) on November 1 and 2. Families go to cemeteries to visit the graves of their loved ones. They clean tombstones, sing songs, and have a feast. But despite the focus on death, it's not a sad time—it's more like a joyful family reunion.

To celebrate Día de Muertos, stores sell edible candy skulls, and people often paint their faces to look like skulls.

HUNGRY GHOST FESTIVAL

Many people in China, Southeast and East Asia celebrate the Hungry Ghost Festival in the seventh month of the lunar calendar, which usually falls in July or August. They believe that ghosts come out from the spirit realm and walk the land. People burn incense and leave out food offerings. At mealtimes, they may leave an empty seat for a dead ancestor.

PITRU PAKSHA

Halloween is only one day, but the Hindu festival of Pitru Paksha lasts for 16! Celebrated in September and October, it is a time when ancestors are believed to visit their families on Earth. People remember their loved ones by praying and leaving food offerings.

OBON

Every summer, people in Japan celebrate Obon, when the spirits of their loved ones are believed to return to the world to visit. In addition to visiting graves and making food offerings, people perform special dances called *bon odori*.

Another celebration in Asia is called the Tomb-Sweeping Festival, when people visit their loved ones' graves.

At the end of the Obon festival, people release floating lanterns into rivers and seas to guide the spirits back to their own world.

45

Quiz

You've made it to the end of the book without getting spooked. Now try this quiz to see how much you remember about Halloween!

1. What do you call a place where pumpkins are grown and picked?

2. What do children often say when they knock on doors on Halloween?

3. True or false: at a trunk-or-treat, you get candy out of a treasure chest?

4. What vegetables are traditionally carved to make jack-o'-lanterns?

5. What is the name of the Celtic festival that Halloween is based on?

6. What festival do many Christians celebrate on November 1?

7. Where was Samhain first celebrated?

8. Why did people start wearing costumes at Samhain?

9. What does the Spanish name *Día de Muertos* mean?

10. Why do people release floating lanterns during the Obon festival?

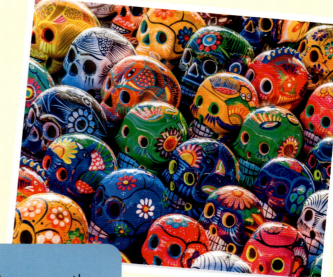

Answers on the next page!

Answers

1. A pumpkin patch

2. "Trick or treat!"

3. False: at a trunk-or-treat, people hand out candy from the trunks of their cars

4. Now people usually carve pumpkins, but in the past, they used turnips, beets, or other large root vegetables

5. Samhain

6. All Saints, also known as All Hallows

7. Ireland and Scotland

8. To confuse evil fairies who might try to kidnap them

9. Day of the Dead

10. To guide the spirits of dead ancestors back to their own world